Views of the sea from the mountaintop

Mayank Mohan Pande

BookLeaf Publishing

India | USA | UK

This book is dedicated to my wife Jaishri, who prompted me to write it and gave general guidance on the themes, to my daughter Bhavya for critical reviews, my son Manu, for his solid all-round support especially for introducing me to many spiritual truths, and late pets, our jet-black labrador Eskimo and beagle Darwin, who made our life's journey secure, full of love, adventure and bliss.

Acknowledgements

I am very grateful to my parents, siblings, in-laws, wife Jaishri, daughter Bhavya, son Manu, late pets Eskimo and Darwin, friends, teachers in school, college, graduate school and employers for having nurtured my creative abilities and giving me the environment for acquiring the best professional knowledge and skills.

I also thank the ONGC, my second employer, for having made possible a healthy and happy family life for us at Dehradun, Nazira in Assam (where it published my first few poems), Ahmedabad, Mumbai and Pune. Credit goes to my instructors and mentors in the Indian Army, my first employer, for exposing me to the art of brevity in writing. Last, but not the least, I am obliged to doctors for their healing touch and regular support.

Preface

I was an avid and regular reader of Norman Vincent Peale's book: 'The Treasury of Courage and Confidence'. It was an anthology of inspiring passages and verses. Over the years I discovered that I too could write pieces with sense and rhyme.

While we were posted in the ONGC Assam headquarters at Nazira from 1994-97, I felt that matters long overdue for writing could be composed with brevity and focus in the form of poems.

Gradually they grew up as a collection and on my father's 100th birth anniversary on 15 Dec 2022, we published a book of my poems entitled 'Memories and Insights'. It contained pieces of recently researched and assembled poems on demystifying radio waves, for instance, amongst many older compositions.
The pace of my writing had slowed down, but Jaishri kept encouraging me. I was also inspired by Mr Ruskin Bond and his book on

the 'Golden Years' as he is 21 years older to me. Thus, when my wife urged me to enter this daily poem-writing event I eagerly did so. At this pace, I'm finding it possible to convert our recent and not-so-recent experiences, observations and thoughts into rhythmically expressed words.

His last teardrop

Darwin our Beagle died at eleven,

His jest for life and his expressions of love
were not dampened by cancer even.

Endure he did pain and discomfort towards
his end,

He let us know WE were his pets and he was
just for our family a godsend.

Our loving friend made us travel by road to
scenic and joyful stations that Mumbai does
surround.

The handsomest of all creatures, wherever we
halted admirers he found.

Struck by partial paralysis early in life, he
recovered much and into cheerfulness his
spirits always did soar.

He gave unconditional love to our family and
all of us loved him evermore.

When his time came to depart, he writhed in
pain and tumours in his ears did crop,

We suffered with him, till he let go and
peacefully slumped, before shedding a
sorrowful teardrop.

He was heartbroken at leaving us just as we
are at the separation, aware, one day, each of
us will also depart sobbing in grief,

Realising we must follow Darwin's example of
loving and being loved before we go, because
a lifetime is not brief.

As winter looms ahead

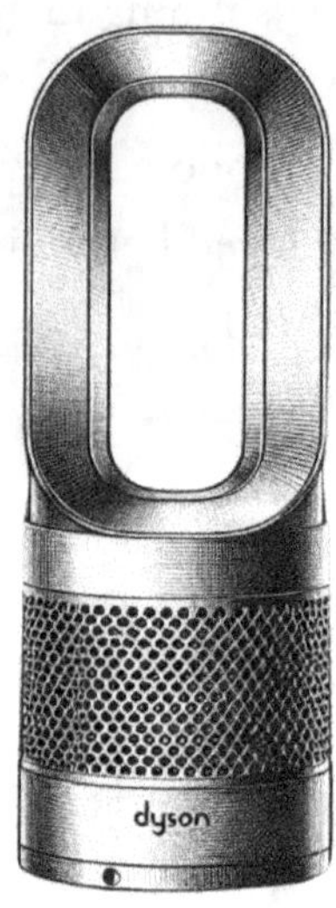

Deepawali swept by and the winter looms
ahead,
And the worsening of air quality we fear and
dread.

It is for the sake of respiratory health,

Which in totality is the only true wealth.

As the air cools in the atmosphere above,

Water vapour condenses on particulate
matter, making smog which falls to the
ground, threatening the lungs of those we
love.

But then science and technology have been
very kind,

Pushing all ill health far behind.

With the air conditioner filtering the dust
and cooling our living room,

Aided by the Dyson air purifier which sweeps
up toxic gases and finer dust like a magic
broom.

The displays go green – signalling good air
quality inside,

Despite the moderate to poor quality of the
air outside.

All the world needs is electricity, which helps
us surmount the heavy odds of keeping our
air clean,

Let us pray that very soon power generation
will itself be inexpensive and green.

Through forested valleys to the sea

For my daughter's birthday, from Pune to
Dapoli in our car, we ventured out,

Which was through forested valleys to the
coast - 180 kms about.

For being careful and knowledgeable
Mangesh, as the driver we chose,

He grew up at Hotel Prospect, Panchgani, a
place which to our hearts and Pune was close.

Hyundai i20 was our car,

Over the last two years, it has taken us afar.

We connected my iPhone to the i20's
infotainment system through the Bluetooth,

This has to be done when the car is stationary,
so that the journey is joyful and smooth.

We halted for breakfast at Mulshi, which
presented of the beautiful lake a tranquil
view,

Ventured ahead and guidance from the car's
navigation system did pursue.

Soon the internet in our mobiles disappeared
because of the dense foliage along the route,

A little uncertainty crept in, the music went
mute.

The car's navigation maps remained accurate,
much to our relief.

In the Lord, and Mangesh's plus my skill and
tech savviness was strengthened our belief.

Our destination 'Saffron Stays Villa 270°' had
not been updated in the maps of our 2020
model car,

Though we always knew our location, we
needed to have a route map lest we drift afar.

Fortunately, Mangesh had entered our destination in Google Maps when our journey had begun,

The route had been displayed because 'Saffron Stays Villa 270°' was only one.

Google Maps showed us our position all along the course,

Helping us to take the correct turn whenever the road did fork.

For a brief time when the internet appeared, I downloaded many a Kishore Kumar song,

And merrily we went up and down scenic forested valleys to climb a sea-facing mountain where history lovers throng.

Pebbles Urbania

We have been here since the second of May,

Mindfulness, my wife pointed out, was a great way.

Thich Naht Hahn on Audible and print,

Offering peace of mind all along and many a hint.

Pune offers coolness and fresh air,

Mindful eating of healthy plus tasty food,
which my daughter designs and my wife does
prepare.

A walking track in the garden below,

Ensures regular physical exercise, leading to
fitness and driving away blues plus any other
woe.

Finding out...

One thing I am very grateful about,

Is my daughter's gift of Feynman's book: 'The pleasure of finding things out'

I am very lucky without a doubt,

And now I write softly instead of loudly shout.

View of the sea from the mountaintop

As we drove up the hill to 'Saffron Stays 270°' in Harnai,

Our eyes beheld a sight that filled us with awe and joy.

A vast expanse of the Arabian Sea,

The Suvarnadurg island fort, surrounded by a coastline with a sea view of near 270 degree.

The sound of waves hitting the shore,

Mingled with those of prayers from
loudspeakers of a temple and mosque below,
plus more.

Which were echoes from the past; of cannons
in ships with sails,

Of Shivaji Maharaj and his Navy braving
colonial invaders and gales...

Walk along...

These are musings on daily walking which brightens the mood with cheerful hues,

It also strengthens the body and banishes the blues.

Releases happiness hormones in the brain,

The bones, joints, heart and digestion also positively gain.

I started many years ago prompted by
doctors, friends and my loving wife,

And hope all will bring it to their routines to
enjoy a long and healthy life...

On giving advice...

O Lord, gratitude to you I extend,

For family, health, happiness, deep listening
and towards service to bend.

Currently, the need for harmony I sense,

I will not give advice and to that of others my
ears will dispense.

Dear Ija (my mother) always cautioned on
giving advice,

Improving only oneself, the setting of an
example will suffice.

One cannot change one's order of birth,

But with our adult ego, respond and keep a
place for mirth...

Gratitude and bliss

We were in Panchgani to celebrate my 69th birthday,

The driver, Mangesh, took us to the plateau 'Table Top' which from Hotel Prospect was not far away,

To see wildflowers, feel the cool breeze on our cheeks and walk because ours was a short stay.

With wild blooms and grass, a solitary tree in the distance,

My daughter with joy ran along the trail
ahead and began to dance with exuberance.

The area had a perimeter of around two miles,

Soon we lost our way and vanished our smiles.

We found a horse trail which because of the
rain,

Had become wet and a muddy plain.

I tried to jump over a slushy patch,

When my right 'slip in' Skechers shoe let go of
my foot, whereas it the mud did catch.

There was no one in sight but we looked
around,

Soon the figure of a man in the distance
noticed our waving hands and towards us was
bound.

An old man in his late fifties reached us when
for the sunset half an hour did remain,

Held each of us in turn by the hand and
helped us to cross over to firm terrain.

This angel did not accept a monetary reward,

Just mentioned he worked in 'Tiger Cave'
restaurant which was a few hundred yards to
the right of the way forward.

We drove back to Hotel Prospect and
witnessed the setting sun and the horizon
kiss,

Praying deeply at dusk, thankfully and
experiencing an everlasting bliss.

Dear Ija (mother)

Where the clean waters of the Yamuna leave
the Himalayas and enter the plains,

Kalsi is where we immersed in 2016, my dear
mother's mortal remains.

Incidentally, in 1930, it was here she was born,

Memories of her love, courage, kindness,
humility and knowledge, thousands of hearts
adorn.

Lessons to live by, we learnt at her knee,

She even addressed my difficulty in reading
when in 1982, I was doing my M.E.

'Read by writing it down' is what she said,

'And with thoughts about thinking, you must
not burden your head'.

Thank you, dear mother, for all your loving
gifts,

Your memory moistens my eyes but spirits
uplifts.

The safe steps of a robot

A little more than 30 years ago,

At the KDMIPE, ONGC, manual handling of hydrofluoric acid, it was desired to forgo.

This was because it's a very hazardous substance,

From our eyes, it especially needed to be kept at a distance.

Fossilised plants and microorganisms studied
under a microscope helped to determine the
age of a rock,

For this first, the sample was digested by
hydrofluoric acid to remove silicate and other
glassy stock.

After centrifuging the liquid was poured,

With the residue smeared by hand onto the
slide to be prepared.

The Director had in France seen a robot do
the job,

He asked us to try & build one because the
acid could the scientist of her eyesight rob.

A member of the user department a design
did suggest,

Like in a concrete mixer, a container the
silicate from the samples with hydrofluoric
acid would digest.

Then spin along its axis, to centrifuge and the
residue separate,
Which then by tilting decanted the liquid and
the residue a robot arm smeared on a
microscope slide plate.

For control, we used an 8-bit microprocessor,

With micro switches, LED sensors and many
a stepper motor.

This was for us the beginning of our journey,
not an end.

We thank the ONGC and IEEE for making us
towards professionalism bend.

Though only a model, not a working piece, we
could make,

But with encouragement from above the first
steps we did take.

Newton, Galileo, Aristotle...

Let's examine profound knowledge full of use,

In civil construction, vehicular technology, weather forecasting, rocketry, in the ordinary world around us and even as a foundation in matters abstruse.

All understanding descended from experiments and keen observations of Newton and his predecessors like Galileo and Aristotle,

But his summary of the matter of motion did
the modern world most significantly enable.

The three laws of Newton that all movements
govern:

(i)   a stationary body cannot move without
being subjected to a force or a moving one
slows down on its own.

(ii)   a heavier body will need a larger force to
have the same acceleration.

(iii) and lastly, if you push against a body, it
will push back with an equal reaction.

Newtonian mechanics and its applications are
all full of glory,

But we do understand, that is a very long
story.

Who are we?

The external world is perceived only through
our senses, which were by providence lent,

Who within is the perceiver in everyone
present?

All immersed in the universe, the earth, ocean
and sky,

These truths have to be felt and experienced
and not be an answer to many a why?

When all is dissolved and to the Earth we
return,

That is the only reality we learn is certain.
Is life only an illusion?

Even this does not appear to be true, because
the Lord enabled us to use words, think and
reason,

To build, procreate and act according to the
season.

Which depends on the heavens, the oceans,
the Earth and sky and the motion of the air
called wind,

Bringing rain, and all of us into physical
reality from the deep recesses of the mind.

Through words, we perceive the experience of
others of the past and present,

Though this is limited as Huston Smith
pointed out, a dog cannot know a
mathematical truth by its scent.

Warm weather in winter

Because of Cyclone 'Fengal' in the Bay of Bengal,

Winds carried moisture to Pune and the sky became cloudy overall.

This had effects which were two fold,

The nights became warmer and the days less cold.

This is because the clouds were thin,

During daytime, letting the sunshine in.

At night, the heat radiated by the ground got
reflected by the mist,

Driving away the winter chill; this is the gist.

Colour

Every morning a dozen flowers on our
balcony do bloom,

My wife has nurtured them, and they drive
away gloom.

In the winter sun, when on the balcony our
cheeks touch a cool breeze,

With green, yellow, pink, orange and purple
around us, we let the joyous moment freeze.

Beautifully stand the pink roses,

Hibiscus, blue pea, parijaat, adenium,
bougainvillaea, croton and kaner also give
colourful poses.

To propagate life is the flower's duty,

Thus, it and all to do with procreation are full
of beauty.

Eskimo on guard

 Eskimo our first pet was born in Kolkata in
August 1998,

He joined us at Ahmedabad, where he came
by air freight.

At that time, he was one month old,

Throughout his life journey, the jet-black
Labrador was loving and bold.

My wife, daughter, son and I ventured out to
Almora in our Santro,

It was a great car, and we were guarded by
Eskimo.

Excellent air conditioning that could cool as
well as heat,

Comfortable seats, lots of legroom and a great
music system that was difficult to beat.

We would drive from five in the morning to
three in the afternoon, breaking for lunch on
the way,

For reaching Almora we made four of a night
stay.

Once when in the early hours we filled
gasoline,

The attendant turned out to be a crook and
very mean.

Insisted he that a similar Santro had filled
petrol earlier on,

And driven away without paying the bill, so
said the con.

He said a woman who looked like my wife
was in that car and took steps towards our
vehicle, with crime compelled,

As he came closer, he yelled out of fear when
he saw Eskimo's eyes, his throat beheld.

The rest of the journey was music and
laughter,

Thanks to Eskimo, to my wife, son and my
daughter.

The fear of death

Death is so certain, and it all do fear,

Especially when danger or old age appear.

The daily newspaper, every morning, the passing away of a few young people in accidents does narrate,

We grimace in fear imagining the situation to be in a bad state.

Not realising that for every loss on the roads,
millions made it to their homes,

The law of averages assures us modern travel
has very safe outcomes.

The credit for this wisdom to Dale Carnegie
does go,

Now let us turn to Adyashanti to further
address our woe.

Fear is a positive emotion as it makes us alert
when in danger,

But if with no peril before us, the feeling does
linger:

Then it is no threat to our lives that we have
to pay attention,

But to fear of the unknown coupled with a gloomy imagination.

If we reflect on the question of who we are?

We see the unknown to be ourselves within, and not far.

And for those who are afraid of pain in the pyre,

A psychiatrist had to say that after death, there is no sensation, even if the body is engulfed by fire.

The daily crossword

The crossword puzzle from 'The Economic Times' every day, I have solved,

Ever since screens began hurting, to use mostly the printed Oxford dictionary and thesaurus, I have resolved.

The puzzle has been taken from 'The Daily Mail',

It straightens reason, builds vocabulary, expands knowledge and relaxes without fail.

Firstly, the anagrams we have to focus and
bring in range,

Here the clue has a group of words containing
the letters to arrange.

This opens the crossword, both columns and
rows,

As a hound sniffs out a trail with his nose.

Have a rubber in your pencil to erase any
answer that is not confirmed by the clue,

Because it will block further solutions which
are unique, not a few.

There are a few other tricks that help relieve
the pressure,

That leads to answers, which is a triumphant
pleasure.

Writer means 'me' the puzzle solver,

Agent means 'spy', 'OR' a soldier.

Then there are words like Paul and pall,
which sound the same but have meanings
disjointed,

One is the answer and to the other, the clue is
pointed.

I'm grateful to my younger brother for
teaching me this art 45 years back,

It has made thinking logical plus pleasurable,
which jumping to conclusions does totally
lack.

The Pune chill

The Pune chill, of Nainital does remind,

Seven months ago, we left the bustling
though packed Mumbai behind.

To a more spacious apartment we shifted,

'Agarwal Packers and Movers' our belongings
safely and swiftly lifted.

Easy for my daughter to commute, no
distance very far,

No mosquitoes do bite, even if the balcony
door is ajar.

Good air quality, ample green space in which
to walk,

An old friend nearby with whom I get to
meet and talk.

In memoriam

The love, care & instruction received from my
near ones departed,

Including my teachers who shaped me right
from 1960, when my schooling started.

Bring back memories of love, commitment
and grace,

Love could be a tough one, but we remember
the givers with gratitude and a smiling face.

First, my dear mother and my kindergarten
teachers who taught me how to pray,

The Irish Christian Brothers, who stressed on
morals, studies and most importantly play.

Reading, writing, arithmetic were given
emphasis,

My dear father added calculus to the learning
and my life became my own thesis.

I followed my elder brother to college, he was
one & a half years older than me,

He exposed me to hard travel that got me
from two institutions each, a degree.

To my dear little sister who passed very
recently,

I have of being cheered out of a depression
and her kindness, a fond memory.

My wife's Dadi, parents and elder brother
who have to heaven gone,

After instructing me with mantras and
lessons on life which my soul adorns.

My Nani I remember for prescribing a good
night's sleep,

Valuable advice because she was a physician's
wife who could laugh as well as weep.

In the end, we remember our pets Eskimo
and Darwin, one of the labrador and the
other of the beagle variety,

Both gave us unconditional love and ensured
all behaviour to be of propriety.

Baby elephant talk

Frightful reports of human-wildlife conflict
in the news regularly appear,

But when the rescue of a group of jumbos
with a baby was featured, it brought in much
great cheer.

The group of 4 with the calf in a pond got
trapped, and when they could not get out
they trumpeted,

This was in a village near Jorhat and the
headman by their calls was alerted.

The men decided to dig on the edges of the
pond to make a gentler slope,

And as they made progress through the night,
it raised everyone's hope.

In the morning, when the calf climbed out,
followed by the adults, they trumpeted in
gratitude, there was no longer in their call
any traces of fear,

Pondering over this one thing is clear:

Humans need animals and plants, and vice
versa, to maintain in nature a perfect balance,

Which appears to be the purpose of
providence...

A letter from my dear mother

Where are you dear Ija (mother)?

We found a 28-year-old letter from you and no other,

Written to us when we were in Nazira, Assam,

And you, Baba (my father) and Shubha (my sister) had gone for a month to Ranichauri in

the hills because Rishikesh had become very
sultry and warm.

I sigh in sorrow because I want to reply to
your letter in detail,

Alas all physical media are bound to fail.

Because the 3 of you are no more,

Baba went in 2002 at 80, you at 86 in 2016 and
Shubha at 61 in early 2024.

There are so many things I want to write to
you about,

About the clarity I have achieved on topics in
childhood I had many a doubt.

One was the unity in matters spiritual,

It took me almost 50 years; understanding
was very gradual.

The other was the question: 'What is money'?

I had posed this to myself in college but could
not find explanations any.

When you came to know with what I was
perplexed,

You had said 'Son, money is what money does.
You should have asked me instead
of breaking your head'.

It was then that I realised the meaning of
'what'?

The answer comes from observation and not
thought.

So dear mother, wherever you are,

Be happy your lessons have been effective,
and
your descendants travelled far.

Studies with my daughter

30 years ago, in a cosy quarter of the ONGC in Nazira, Assam,

My sweet daughter sought my help in her studies not because they were bothersome,

But because she was curious with a yearning for knowledge and wisdom.

She showed me in her social studies book the
lesson she had to prepare,

It was about a country which was called Zaire
and of which I was unaware.

Out came the Oxford School Atlas and we
began to explore,

Got to know about its history and geography
plus a lot more.

It had a drawing of the solar system which the
seasons did explain,

The tilt in the Earth's axis of rotation as it
revolved around the sun is what made the
matter plain.

Thank you Ija (mother)

Bhagwan Shri Ramana Maharshi beckoned us
down South,

His thoughts were known to us in letters as
also by word of mouth.

At the holy resort, Sparsa, we lodged,

For us to visit the temple, Ramana Ashram
and the drive around Arunachala Hill an auto
At 0500 hours, they engaged.

We drove down and looked up at the tall
temple structure with deities carved in stone,

My wife, daughter and I queued up for
darshan of the deity as there were hundreds
who
had come from afar for the purpose; we were
not alone.

A sadhu came and applied sandalwood paste
and sacred ash on the forehead,

And the queue slowly, steadily barefooted
inched forward.

Diyas with their wicks dipped in ghee, added
to the divine glow,

And systematically in 2 hours, all proceeded
out in a smooth flow.

As my daughter again queued up to buy

prasad,

I stood restlessly because I was tired and
hungry, and wanted to go back to where we
had lodged.

There were three crowded benches,
All the rest were standing.

It was then that I saw a mother on the bench
her baby breastfeeding.

She beckoned me to come and sit beside her
and made space in her bench,

She communicated in a divine language, not
English or French.

We could visit Ramana Maharshi ashram, buy
priceless books and drive around the holy
mountain, inspired and cleaned in every way,

It was then I realised your presence, dear mother, because it was your birthday.

Swings

Ups and downs in my life, I have seen,

Confident at times, down in between.

But then I was trained to persevere,

Not to give in, in any situation anywhere.

Also in the Holy Geeta I had read, feelings
arise from the senses and are transient,

They come and go; just must be bravely
resilient.

But because bipolar disorder was in my genes,

Reading was supplemented by a mild dose of
medicines.

My wife, daughter, son and pets were always
in support,

Making life more blissful than any I had
thought.

www.ingramcontent.com/pod-product-compliance
Lightning Source LLC
Chambersburg PA
CBHW072048150726

47996CB00015B/2236